Speak to My Heart

Pathway's of Prophesy

Anthony KaDarrell Thigpen

Library of Congress Cataloging-in-Publication Data

Anthony KaDarrell Thigpen
Literacy in Motion Publications

Speak to My Heart

ISBN: 978-0-9777697-5-9

1. Christians - Religious Life
Printed in the United States of America

Published by
Literacy in Motion
PO BOX 7186
Chandler, AZ 85246
posttribune@hotmail.com
KaDarrell@sbcglobal.net

Prophet: (Hebrew) *Navi*; fruit of the lips.

There are forty-eight male prophets recorded in the sixty-six canonical books of the Holy Bible. There are also seven females identified as prophetesses. Interestingly, there is only one recorded Gentile prophet referenced. The hundreds of other prophets mentioned in the Bible are defined as false prophets. Very few people have been privileged, humbled and acknowledged for speaking on behalf of The Creator.

4-STEPS TO DISTINGUISHING GOD'S VOICE

1.   THE **NATURE** OF HOW THE CREATOR SPEAKS...
"And after the earthquake a fire; but the Lord was not in the fire: and after the fire a *STILL SMALL VOICE*" (II Kings 19:12).

2.   THE **PRE-REQUISITE** OF HEARING GOD SPEAK...
"That I may know him, and the power of his resurrection, and *THE FELLOWSHIP OF HIS SUFFERINGS*, being made conformable unto his death" (Philippians 3:10).

3.   THE **PROMISE** OF WHEN THE CREATOR SPEAKS...
"But thou art holy, O thou that *INHABITEST THE PRAISES* of Israel," (Psalms 22:3).

4.   THE **ASSURANCE** OF WHAT HAPPENS WHEN THE CREATOR STILL SPEAKS...
"So shall my word be that goes forth out of my mouth: it shall not return unto me void, but **it shall accomplish that which it please, and it shall prosper** in the thing whereto I send it," (Isaiah 55:11).

DISPELLING COMMON MYTHS

"God said..."

"Then the Lord said unto me, the prophets prophesy lies in my name: I sent them not, neither have I commanded them, neither spoke unto them: they prophesy unto you a false vision and divination, and a thing of naught, and the deceit of their heart" (**Jeremiah 14:14**).

"God still speaks..."

"Think not that I am come to destroy the law, or the prophets: I am not come to destroy, but to fulfill" (**Matthew 5:17**).

"New Testament Prophets under the New Covenant..."

"And he gave some, apostles; and some, prophets; and some, evangelists; and some, pastors and teachers" (**Ephesians 4:11**).

DEDICATION

This book is dedicated to pathfinders. Your suffering has purpose. Your frustrations and failures will end in continued favor. You are not alone. Your tribulation is merely a pathway to prophesy.

Content

INTRODUCTION

Avoid Sensationalism

GOD HAS AN IDENTITY

Most people are spiritually asleep or unconscious. There are also those that claim and/or aim to walk by faith, but often find themselves sleepwalking. Organized religion has the potential to provide a positive impact on communities, cities, and even countries – sometimes it does. Unfortunately, all too often it does not. Therefore, we must caution ourselves. Organized religion often fosters a false sense of individual identity and artificial spirituality. When prayer, worship, and praise is limited to isolated services it fosters an inauthentic and disingenuous 21st century concept of situational spirituality.

What if no one ever told you there was a God, or if there was no Bible or scrolls? We would have no other choice except to introspectively search within ourselves. Instead, throughout history, kingdoms have created and defined ideas and interpretations with the end goal redefining the Creator's identity. Mankind has aimed to define, name, and brand God in order to fulfill their own selfish ambitions. We've defined doctrines that best fit the circumstances, conveniences and advancement of societies, communities and cultures in which we live. Absent of these antics and uncertain beliefs the Creator remains the same yesterday, today, and forever. An atheist cannot erase the Creator's identity; an agnostic cannot lessen it; no more than a believer can change or manipulate it.

Throughout history, religion has given the Creator gender specific titles, subjective books and theories to accommodate and validate different regions around the world. Religion also outlines doctrines that define organized hierarchy. Even still, the "Great I Am" remained unchanged. Despite mankind's efforts to manipulate and control the masses, God still speaks. C. S. Lewis in *Mere Christianity* defines the *Natural Law* as the law in our hearts. He says, all of humanity acknowledges "right vs. wrong." People all over the earth believe we are supposed to behave a certain way, even when we don't. Lewis makes it clear that he is not referring to learned behavior or human instincts. The Natural Law illustrates that we are not just being human, much rather we are spiritual-beings. This is why it's important to objectively search within to discover truth. Likewise, the Creator is a spirit, who is neither male nor female, superior to all that is, and omnipresent and omniscient.

As expected, every religion defines whom they worship as the God of all gods. However, embracing doctrines and protocols will never be as fulfilling as embodying truth. Simply stated, religion is merely a way of life, which involves beliefs and systems that explain the origin of life on earth and after death. Every religion seems to possess enlightening aspects that make people feel closer to the deity they worship. It's important to remain open to gaining knowledge and understanding about life. Otherwise, we will not grow spiritually. We grow through the process of thinking, learning, believing and understanding.

Most importantly, growth will not and cannot happen without the brave heart to unlearn cultural traditions that were invented to promote superiority.

When this process happens, we no longer need to blindly believe what faith has already proven. I used to believe I would one day get married and have a child. After marriage, I became the proud father of a beautiful daughter. That blind belief is no longer necessary – reality has erased all uncertainties and my hope is fulfilled. An inward glance at our life's journey of successes and failures, misfortunes and celebrations, even losses and gains, enable us to see a glimpse of God's identity.

GOD HAS A NAME

As a child, I used to think that John 11:35 was the saddest scripture in the Bible, "Jesus wept." As an adult, the most devastating and frightening verse is Matthew 24:1, "Jesus left." The absence of eternal salvation, life after death, or religion as we know it, poses fear. That mere thought causes people to avoid asking necessary questions about God and His identity. I don't blame you for avoiding the difficult questions, and ignoring thoughts that will undoubtedly lead to deeper levels of consciousness. It's much easier to just go along with the status quo. As I continued praying, meditating, studying and searching, living my life in darkness stopped being an option. As a result, I started examining and asking the kind of questions that left me feeling isolated. The more I sought the truth, the more religious leaders started pushing me away. It started when I asked one simple question, "Does God have a name, and if so, why don't we use it?"

The title, "God" is an improper noun that can be affixed to any deity. It is an expression of what one is, more than who they are. There are many people who have the titles Mr., Mrs., Ma'am or Sir, but the name behind the title is where the true meaning stems. As it relates to identity, names are important. The proper name of a person, place or thing marks significance. As created beings, we do not have the knowledge or wherewithal to mark God's identity in totality. Therefore, Moses, a patriarch of believers, who is said to have gained a glimpse of God's identity, shared an irrefutable truth. God Himself gave Moses His proper name. Moses repeated that name as "Yah." In English, Yah is interpreted "I AM." Yah is the only name without limitations, restrictions, or boundaries. It is all encompassing. Hence, *Halle Lu Jah*, which are three Hebrew words meaning "Praise You Yah," is a biblical reference sited as the highest praise. An unknown author once said, *"Remember that a man's name to him is the sweetest most important sound in any language."* According to the Bible, there is nothing greater, and no praise higher, then exalting God by His name – *Halle Lu YAH*!

LOST IN TRANSLATION

There are so many faulty translations in the Bible, but the truth remains unchanged. Without having to debate, I understand who people are referring to when they say and sing about God or Jesus. What I don't think they understand is why God's name is never used during their time of alleged intimate worship. It's like calling your spouse, "Wife or Husband" during intimate moments. Christ's name is Yahshua. Everything about his life intentionally gives Yah glory. Ultimately, his name means "I AM is salvation". The meaning of His name is often lost in translation and transliteration, originally with intent, presently out of ignorance. Approximately in the 16th century, European-speaking cultures changed Yahshua to Jesus – a name more fitting to the dominance and advancement of Western civilizations.

Transliteration of Yahshua into Jesus

YAH	SH	UA	Hebrew
IE	S	OUS	Greek
IE	SO	US	Latin
JE	S	US	English

The letter "Y" was transliterated to the letter "J," specifically as it relates to names in Latin and English Bibles. This cast dark shadows over significantly understanding the source of Christian influence. The Bible is a good book, and remains a great resource for students and researchers who dig deep beyond the surface of the letter. However, all believers need to learn how to rely on the source of the living God. Instead, far too many Christians are hypnotized by false interpretations and transliterations of the Bible. *Speak to My Heart* will help readers use the Bible as a resource to discover pathways to knowing and experiencing the great "I AM" on a personal level.

CHURCH SERVICES SHOULD ME MORE THAN SENSATION

One of the most controversial issues that cause individuals to discredit Christianity is false prophesy. It ruins lives, controls individuals through manipulation, and discourages attendance to general assemblies. So many churchgoers, especially in the Pentecostal movement have confused sanctification with sensationalism. The tingle, twitch, tongues, and tears, despite how refreshing or exhilarating, are no indication of a true move of God. When worshippers shout, shuffle their feet, or sing with passion, these are not concrete indications of the glory manifested by God's presence. When worship is reduced to mere sensationalism, our emotions prevent us from hearing and hiding God's genuine message in our hearts. While believers are encouraged to make a joyful noise and shout praises, we must be careful not to confuse sensation and inspiration with revelation and relationship. This book is not a commentary nor a narrative intended to serve as another crutch or a guide. Neither is this book a substitute for Spirit given to comfort, lead, teach and guide. *Speak to My Heart* is a letter that has been separated into ten sections to illustrate what the Bible actually says about prophecy, the voice of God, and the characteristics of how God speaks.

THEY USE, "GOD SAID" TO ADVANCE THEIR OWN AGENDAS

It is common for many churchgoers, especially spiritual leaders, to use the expression "God said" to validate their own personal agendas. When I was about 22-years-old, in 1992, after returning from the frontlines of the Iraq War, I was honorably discharged from the Army. At the time, I had no clue what I wanted to do with my life. Anger from childhood disappointments kept me from returning home. The guilt that comes with killing in a war kept me from advancing forward. I had no vision for my life. I was stuck. I faithfully served in a well-established Pentecostal church, living paycheck to paycheck, uneducated, with no personal ambitions other than routine involvement in weekly church services. During this challenging season of my life, the bishop told me that "God said," a certain woman was my wife. By then, I'd seen miracles happen in that church. I'd witnessed powerful acts of exorcism and deliverance. Yet, when the commandment to wed a woman that I hardly even knew echoed over the pulpit, confusion controlled the circumstance. "Why hadn't God told me this," I asked myself repeatedly? I painfully pursued the relationship with uncertainties, hoping to please God, amid an already disappointed bishop who wanted me to blindly obey. During an evening worship service, ministers were instructed to form a line, and one-by-one more than 30 preachers publically scolded me with harsh scriptures, theatrically and aggressively rebuking my disobedience. I was crushed. Each rebuke that echoed over the pulpit shattered my heart into unidentifiable pieces. Soon after, I was lost, broken, and engaged, but certainly not in love. It was a short-lived engagement. I formed a close friendship with the God-fearing young lady prior to relocating to a different region. I managed to escape that particular church and false prophesy that nearly ruined my life. I never looked back. The devil comes only to kill, steal, and destroy. Those false words, "God said," were intended to steal my free will and destroy my destiny. Had I submitted, I would have had no more life in me than a mere puppet. Leaders who use the expression, "God said", loosely are under the devil's influence, and may not even realize it. These words are often used to advance selfish agendas. Perhaps we would have made a great couple within an arranged marriage, but I have no regrets. No relationship is worth allowing another individual to manipulate and control your destiny.

Critical thinking, personal study, and deep mediation seem to have no place in religion today, especially amongst lay members. Christ had 12 disciples. 'Disciple' is the root word of discipline. The word literally means learner, student, and philosopher. Critical thinking played a significant role in the early church, in so much that the Roman (European) Empire declared public assembly forbidden until the 4th century. Many corrupt religious leaders despise free will and choice. They control their parishioners with manipulative influences. Much like slave traders during the 300 years of the Transatlantic Slave Trade. Sadly, corrupt church pastors share similar strategies. They misuse scriptures and twist the truth to force submissive followers to obey, with limited emphasis placed on God's will. How can you obey God, if you have no clue as to how He speaks, and what His voice sounds like when He does? People with good intentions who fail to hear God's voice often follow men or rebel against the discovery of truth.

WHEN MEN RULE MEN

Much like the Israelites wanted a King to rule over them, men and women today, still search for pastors to rule over their personal matters. In other words, people exalt religious leaders to the extent of poisoning pastors with an overdose of power. It's been said time and time again, that absolute power corrupts absolutely. As a result, such leaders lie on God in effort to gain greater influence, sustain their position of power, and wage more respect. It is sensationalism at its best. Some sensationalists are absolutely persuaded that they are hearing from God, when in fact, they are consumed by their own subconscious thoughts. The term "God said" has become a repetitive and misused cliché. The scripture warns against such behavior. *"Then the Lord said unto me, The prophets prophesy lies in my name: I sent them not, neither have I commanded them, neither spoke unto them: they prophesy unto you a false vision and divination, and a thing of naught, and the deceit of their heart"* (Jeremiah 14:14). As a result of this ever-growing deceptive disease of lying on the Great I AM, churchgoers must take painstaking precautions. It is important for the religious community to understand Yah's word and His intentions. Interestingly enough, the expression "God said" is not used in any scripture amongst New Testament (NT) believers. While Old Testament (OT) patriarchs used such language by necessity, NT believers have reduced the notion to sensationalism. Unequivocally, God continues to speak. However, how He speaks is the subject of this next lesson.

WHAT CHANGED FROM THE OLD TESTAMENT TO NOW?

Under the OT covenant our relationship with God was communal, as in community-based. The NT covenant enables and encourages believers to establish individual relationships. This mean that God would often speak audibly under the old covenant, and He speaks to the hearts of men under the new covenant. Ultimately, God's intentions do not change. It has always been His desire to hide His message in the hearts of His people, regardless of the covenant dispensation (see Psalms 119:11). As a result, He speaks with a *still small voice* (see I Kings 19:12). Unfortunately, far too many people fail to recognize the Voice of God. Therefore, they depend on others to communicate messages from-and-to God – this is dangerous. While five-fold ministry has a critical place in our lives, it is God's intent that His relationship with mankind remains personal and free will. *Speak to My Heart* will help readers/thinkers put personal relationship and public worship in proper perspectives.

The theme of Jesus' entire ministry was centered on bridging the gap and mending a relationship between God and mankind. He tore the holy veil that once served as a partition symbolizing the of separation between God and mankind. Despite this reality, far too many Christians continue to seek the psychological, emotional, and spiritual guidance of religious leaders. These leaders are the men and women called spiritual mothers and fathers. However, our only spiritual Father is God Himself, all others are insufficient substitutes. Once believers accept this reality, they will no longer need to depend on mere men to play the role of God in their personal lives (see John 16:13 and I John 2:27). Religious leaders will best serve their purpose when they operate in the humility wherewith they are called.

BEWARE OF MANIPULATION

As a result of believers failing to study, refusing to pray, and forgetting to simply put God first, many are manipulated. Manipulation is trickery used to pollute and contaminate an environment. Consider the phonics when examining the prefix, root, and suffix of any word, man\i\pulate. Witchcraft, sorcery, false prophesy and manipulation are all weapons the enemy uses to combat truth. Leadership is important. However, corrupt leadership is the mastermind behind manipulation. (See: Ephesians 4:12). This happens every time one individual is given absolute power, because absolute power corrupts absolutely.

The enemy aims to destroy every prophet, distract every messenger, and muzzle every mouthpiece? There is something extremely unique about the office of the prophet that is often overlooked. According to the words of Amos 3:7, "Surely the Lord God will do nothing, but He revels his secret unto His servants the prophets." Hence, prophets gauge when God will act.

Every prophet serves as both a mouthpiece for God and a seer. They are often despised as rebels and assassinated. Their messages bring no self-glory or personal gain. They are not faultless - they possess the same frailties as other human beings. The prophet sees, warns, declares, defies, instructs, redirects, and ultimately speaks on behalf of God. Understanding the office of a prophet and the gifts of prophesy will help individuals prepare themselves for spiritual warfare. It will also help believers avoid the kinds of manipulation that ruin lives, destroy marriages, and pollute sound doctrine.

HOW DO YOU KNOW IF GOD SAID IT?

How do we distinguish between God's voice, our own consciousness, peer pressure, and the enemy's negative influences? They all seem to have similarities. For example, they are still small voices. When we audibly speak, human voices travel through sound waves, unlike these inner voices that are without motion, much like thought. When people are diagnosed with mental health conditions like schizophrenia, these individuals specifically hear voices in their head.

'Psychosis' comes from a Greek word meaning "psyche, mind/soul, abnormal condition or derangement." This is what people are called when they have a loss of contact with reality. Such conditions are accompanied with difficult social interaction and impairment to carry out daily life activities. God's voice is not in your head; it's in your heart. He speaks to your spirit. In fact, studies show that hearing voices is a common symptom of severe mental illnesses. Hearing these voices is said to be a very overwhelming experience.

Relationship with God demands periods of isolation, seasons of consecration, and daily moments of meditation. On the contrary, quality human relationships demand communication. We audibly project our voices in effort to be heard. Our words travel through sound waves from one person to another. On the other hand, God's voice is still and small. It has no motion; therefore, it does not travel through sound waves. God's voice is so unique that it requires mediation during our prayer, praise and worship experience in effort to be experienced. People who meditate on wickedness do the deeds thereof. People who meditate consciousness are self-centered, usually focused on self-image, and promote messages of self-love. Believers who mediate on the Great I Am deny themselves, and forsake their own worldly ambitions. If there is no suffering, sacrifice, or obedience involved in your gain, then God's voice is not producing the results. The enemy preys on people who look for shortcuts in life. *Speak to My Heart* will sharpen your spiritual vision. If you are in search of the mysteries of God for selfish gain, I warn you not to read another word of this book.

Slave masters imposed translated, transcribed, and transliterated King James Bibles on African servants. They violently forced their Anglo-Saxon pagan practices, culture, customs and confusion on African slaves. As a result, today's Christians do not celebrate Holy/Feast Days. Instead, Christians worldwide commemorate the pagan feasts of "Samhain;" *the festival or season of the dead*. This includes holidays like *Halloween, Christ-Mas, Valentine's Day*, and *Easter*. These religious principals have been defined by racism and paganism and remain unchallenged and repeatedly celebrated. Literary truths have been buried beneath centuries of lies and deception. Yet, God's voice cannot be silenced. Church leaders in Europe established religious dominance by soliciting the support of pagans, compromising the truth, and redefining the Bible for selfish gain. In particularly, Romans stole religious artifacts and literature from the Middle East and Africa, redefined it, and built the world's largest empire based on the religious reform of Christianity. The Bible was also used to prevent slave revolts, and currently used to control the masses, yet it still contains sacred passages to spirituality. As a result, the pursuit of truth requires a complicated mixture. Believers must study, research and 'unlearn' untruths, and unlearning ambiguous discrepancies can be as difficult forward thinking. Most importantly, desperately desiring to hear the voice of God is the ultimate gateway to spirituality, improvement, and truth.

25

Section I

CONCISE SUMMARY

Understanding the 16 Books of Prophesy

The Prophet
Isaiah

(Enduring Rejection)

Historical Summary
ISAIAH (i/zay'/uh) Personal name meaning, "Yahweh saves."
Prophet active in Judah about 740 to 701 B.C.
Wife: Called "The Prophetess" (See: Isaiah 8:3)

The greatest of the known prophets appeared at a critical moment of Israel's history. It was during the second half of the eighth century B.C. that the northern kingdom was conquered by Assyria in 722 B.C. In the year that Uzziah, king of Judah, died in 742 B.C., Isaiah received his call to the prophetic office in the Temple of Jerusalem.

It's important to note that King Uzziah took the throne at age 16, and reigned prosperously about 52 years. During his early years, while under the influence of prophet Zechariah, he was faithful to God. During his reign, he used skillful men to make military machines. He built major cities under his leadership. He refortified the country, reorganized and reequipped the army, and engaged in agricultural endeavors. There was great material prosperity during his reign that distracted God's people from spirituality. King Uzziah's prideful downfall was revealed when he defiantly entered the temple to burn incense on the altar. It wasn't until Uzziah's death that Isaiah saw the Lord sitting upon a throne, high and lifted up. Whatever authority we submit or surrender to, their words have the potential to redefine our destiny. Only allow God to reign as author of your faith. No leader, despite the successes of his/her past, should prevent you from seeing God for who He is. (See: Isaiah 6:11-13 and Ezekiel 28:16). Uzziah reigned from ages 16-68. He attempted to take over the religious rites of the priesthood. He focused on prosperity. The sixth chapter of the book of Isaiah is where his divine summons is described. The glory of the Lord took possession of his spirit.

As a result, Isaiah gained a new awareness of human pettiness and vanity. The enormous abyss between God's sovereignty and man's sin overwhelmed him. Only the purifying coal of the seraphim could cleanse his lips and prepare him for the call: "Here I am, send me!" The life and ministry of Isaiah can be divided into three periods: 1. The reigns of King Jotham 2. King Ahaz, and 3. King Hezekiah. Early prophecies are listed in the first period (Isa 1–5). The book of Isaiah also exposes the moral breakdown of Judah and its capital city, Jerusalem.

With the appointment of Ahaz, the prophet became adviser to the king. (Jotham, the son of Uzziah reigned for 11 years, prior to his son Ahaz). The Ephraimites threatened Ahaz's throne. Ahaz rejected Isaiah's advise for faith and courage and turned to Assyria for help, a colony of Babylon. From this period came the majority of messianic prophecies (Isaiah 6–12). Hezekiah succeeded his father, Ahaz. He undertook the religious reform that Isaiah supported. Unfortunately, the old scheming restarted. Isaiah summoned Judah to faith in God. However, the revolt had already begun. Assyria acted quickly ravaging Judah, and laying siege to Jerusalem. *"I shut up Hezekiah like a bird in his cage,"* boasts the famous inscription of Sennacherib. But God delivered the city, as Isaiah promised. Little is known about the last days of Isaiah. The complete Book of Isaiah is an anthology of poems written primarily by the prophet, but also by his disciples, some of who came many years after Isaiah's death. In chapters 1-39 most of the prophecies come from Isaiah. They reflect the situation in eighth-century Judah. Disciples are accredited to sections such as the Apocalypse of Isaiah (chapters 24 – 27), the prophecies against Babylon (chapters 13 – 14), and probably the poems of Isaiah (chapters 34 – 35). Chapters 40 – 55, are generally attributed to an anonymous poet. Isaiah 56 – 66 contains later periods and was composed by disciples who inherited the spirit and continued Isaiah's prophetic work as scribes, disciples, and even prophets.

The Prophet
Jeremiah
(Enduring Arrest, Imprisonment and Public Disgrace)

Historical Summary
JEREMIAH (jehr/ih/mi'/uh) Personal name meaning, may Yahweh lift up, found or throw

---

The Book of Jeremiah combines history, biography, and prophesy. It portrays a nation and leader in crisis. Jeremiah was placed with a heavy burden of the prophetic office. He has born about 650 B.C. of a priestly family from the little village of Anathoth, near Jerusalem, a city assigned to the tribe of Benjamin warriors. He was called in his thirteenth year of King Josiah. Josiah's reform begun with enthusiasm and hope, but ended with his death on the battlefield of Megiddo. Josiah was killed attacking the Egyptian Pharaoh Neco. The prophet whole-heartily supported the reform of the pious King Josiah, which began in 629 B.C. Nineveh, the capital of Assyria, fell in 612, preparing the way for the new Babylon, which was soon to put an end to Judean independence. After the death of Josiah the old idolatry returned. Jeremiah suffered arrest, imprisonment, and public disgrace as his lot. Jeremiah is often referred to as the weeping prophet. He also the prophet that saw Judah's doom, the affects of false prophecy, and his own death by his own people. Afterward, Nebuchadnezzar captured Jerusalem and carried King Jehoiachin into exile (see Jeremiah

22:24). During the years 598 – 587 BC, Jeremiah tried to counsel King Mattaniah, who Nebuchadnezzar made Jehoiachin's successor, and gave him a slave name of Zedekiah. Jeremiah ministered to Zedekiah in the face of opposition. The false prophet Hananiah proclaimed that the yoke of Babylon was broken. As a result, Zedekiah revolted. Nebuchadnezzar took swift and terrible vengeance; Jerusalem was destroyed in 587. Its leading citizens were sent into exile. About this time, Jeremiah uttered the prophesy of the "New Covenant" (Jeremiah 31:31-34). The prophet remained in the ruins of Jerusalem, but was later taken into Egyptian exile. While in exile, according to tradition, the prophet was murdered by his own countrymen. However, the influence of Jeremiah was greater after his death. The exiled community read and meditated on the lessons of the prophet. His influence can be seen in the book of Ezekiel, certain of the Psalms, and the second part of Isaiah. Baruch was instrumental in helping Jeremiah to write and speak prophecies from the Lord (see Jeremiah 36). Shortly after the exile, the Book of Jeremiah, as we have it in translation today, was published in a final edition.

The Prophetic Book of
Lamentations

Historical Summary
JEREMIAH (jehr/ih/mi'/uh) Personal name meaning, "May Yahweh lift up," "throw," or "found"

The sixth century B.C. was an age of crisis for Israel. With the destruction of the temple, the exile of the leaders, and loss of national sovereignty, an era ended. Not long after the fall of Jerusalem in 587 B.C., an eyewitness composed these five laments. Greeks often accredit Jeremiah, the weeping prophet, for having written the text. The book includes confession, grief, suffering, humiliation, submission to merited chastisement, and strong faith to restore. The union of agonizing grief with unquenchable hope reflects the constant prophetic vision. This union is a reflection of human weakness and the strength of God's love; it also shows how Israel's faith in Yahweh could survive the shattering experience of national ruin. As a literary work, the Book of Lamentations is carefully constructed. The first four poems are called acrostics, in which the separate stanzas begin with successive letters of the Hebrew alphabet, from the first to the last. In Lamentations, the figure of Israel as the bride of YHWH, is depicted as a desolate widow.

The Prophet
Ezekiel
(First known prophet called in Babylon)

Historical summary
EZEKIEL (e/zee'/kih/ehl) Personal name meaning, "God will strengthen."

Ezekiel resembles the more primitive type of prophet. Much like Elijah and Elisha, he clearly depends on all his predecessors in prophesy, and his teaching is a development of theirs. His unique contribution to the history of prophetism is seen in his interest in the temple. His form of public worship parallels no other prophet, not even Jeremiah, who, like Ezekiel, was also a priest. He is often called the "father of Judaism," and formed a post-exilic religion. We are sure that this book is the prophet's own work, however, edits and additions appear from others who share his interest. Ezekiel became a prophet in Babylon. He is the first known prophet to receive the call to prophesy outside the Holy Land. The first part of his book consists of reproaches for Israel's past. In 587, when Nebuchadnezzar destroyed Jerusalem, Ezekiel was vindicated before his unbelieving fellow citizen. Afterward, Ezekiel's message changes. From then on his prophesy is characterized by the promise of salvation in a new covenant, and he lays down the conditions necessary to obtain it. His final eight chapters are a utopian vision of the Israel of the future. The famous vision of the dry bones in chapter 37 expresses his firm belief in a forthcoming restoration. Ezekiel's new covenant, like Jeremiah's would only see its true fulfillment in the New Testament. Ultimately, Ezekiel declares that whatever God does is motivated by zeal for his own holy name. The new heart and the new spirit, which must exist under the new covenant, cannot be the work of man – They must be the work of God. These teachings helped prepare for the New Testament doctrine of salvation through grace.

The Prophet
Daniel

(An Apocalyptic Book, with an Unknown Author, Named in Honor of Daniel)

Historical Summary
Daniel (dan'iehl) Personal name meaning, "God is judge" or "God's judge."

This book does not take its name from the author, who is actually unknown, but from its hero, a young Jew taken early to Babylon. There are non-canonical writings by a sixth century B.C. prophet named Daniel. The non-canonical (Books not included in the Bible) writings of the actual prophet whose name was Daniel make 2nd Century BC references. Therefore, the NT reference of the Prophet Daniel in the gospel of Matthew (vs.24:15) is not a reference to this apocalyptic writer recorded in the Septuagint. The Septuagint is the oldest Greek version of the Hebrew OT. The book does not actually belong to the prophetic writings, rather to a distinctive type of literature known as apocalyptic. Apocalyptic writing enjoyed its greatest popularity from 200 B.C. to 100 A.D. Apocalyptic literature has its roots in teaching of the prophets, who often pointed ahead to the day of the Lord. This work was composed during the bitter persecution carried on by Antiochus IV Epiphanes from 167-164 B.C. It was intended to strengthen and comfort the Jewish people. The book tells of the trials and triumphs of Daniel and his three companions. The moral is that men of faith can resist temptation and conquer adversity. The book details a series of visions promising deliverance and glory to the Jews. Under this apocalyptic imagery are contained some of the best elements of prophetic teaching: 1. The insistence on right conduct, 2. The divine control over events, and 3. The certainty that the kingdom of God will ultimately triumph. The arrival of the kingdom is a central theme of the synoptic gospels (Matthew, Mark, and Luke), and Christ, in calling himself the "Son of Man," reminds us that He fulfills the destiny of this mysterious figure in the seventh chapter of Daniel.

The Prophet
Hosea

(Married a Prostitute in Obedience to God)

Historical Summary
HOSEA (hoh/ssee'/uh) Personal name meaning, "Salvation."

Hosea belonged to the northern kingdom and began his prophetic career in the last years of Jeroboam II (786 – 746 B.C.). Some believe that he was a priest, others that he was a cult prophet. A cult prophet merely identified his dealings with a specific sect of people. His prophesy is our only source of information concerning his life. The collected prophecies reveal a very sensitive, emotional man who could pass quickly from violent anger to the deepest tenderness. The prophecy pivots around his own unfortunate marriage to Gomer, a prostitute. This was a personal tragedy, which profoundly influenced his teaching. In fact, his prophetic message was deepened by the painful experience he underwent in his married life. Gomer, the adulteress, symbolized faithless Israel. Just as Hosea could not give up his wife, even when she played the harlot, so God could not renounce Israel. God chastises only with the chastisement of jealous lover. God longs to bring people back to their first love. Israel's infidelity took the form of idolatry and ruthless oppression of the poor. No amount of sensationalism, materialism or sacrifices could atone for her sins. Chastisement alone remained; God would have to strip her of the rich ornaments bestowed by her false lovers and thus bring her back to the true lover. A humiliated Israel would again seek God. The eleventh chapter of Hosea is one of the summits of OT theology; God's love for his people is passionately expressed. Hosea spearheaded the tradition of describing the relationship between God and Israel in terms of marriage. This symbolism appears later throughout the Bible.

The Prophet
Joel
(Frightened by What He Witnessed)

Historical Summary
JOEL (joh'ehl) Personal name meaning, "Yah is God."

This prophesy is rich an apocalyptic imagery (widespread devastation) and eschatological tone (doctrine concerning the end-time). It was composed about 853 B.C. The overall theme is the day of the Lord. A terrible invasion of locusts ravaged Judah. The dream was so horrifying that the prophet visualized it as a symbol of the coming day of the Lord. The prophet summoned the people to repent with fasting and weeping. They were ordered to conduct a solemn assembly in which the priests would pray for deliverance. The Lord answered their prayer, promised to drive away the locusts, and to bring peace and prosperity. He also promised an outpouring of the Spirit on all flesh. The concluding poem pictures the nations gathered in the Valley of Jehoshaphat, where the Lord is about to pass judgment. The riotous mass assembled in the valley of decision. The prophecy changes abruptly from the terrifying image of judgment to a vision of Israel restored.

The Prophet
Amos

(Expelled by Royal Sanctuary Priests for Prophesies of Harsh Judgment)

Historical Summary
AMOS (ay'/mahss) Personal name meaning, "a load," nicknamed burden barrier.

Amos was actually a shepherd of Tekoa in Judah, who exercised his ministry during the prosperous reign of Jeroboam II (786-746 B.C.). He prophesied in Bethel, before being expelled by the priest in charge of the royal sanctuary. The poetry of Amos, who denounces hollow prosperity, is filled with imagery and language taken from his own pastoral background. The book is an anthology of his prophecies; they were compiled either by the prophet or by some of his disciples. The prophecy begins with a sweeping indictment of Damascus, Philistia, Tyre, and Edom. When Amos prophesied the overthrow of the sanctuary, the fall of the royal house, and the captivity of the people, it was more than Israeli officials could bear. The priest of Bethel drove Amos away, but not before hearing a horrible prophetic judgment pronounced upon them. Amos is a prophet of divine judgment. The sovereignty of God dominated his thoughts. He was no innovator. He called the people back to the high moral and religious demands of YHWH's revelation. Like other prophets,

40

Amos knew that divine punishment is never completely destructive; it is part of the hidden plan of God to bring salvation to men. Amos' final prophecy opens up a perspective of restoration under King David.

The Prophet
Obadiah

(Nothing Known Except for this Writing of the Shortest and Sternest Prophesy)

Historical Summary
OBADIAH (oh/buh/di'/uh) Personal name meaning, "Yahweh's servant."

The twenty-one verses of this book contain the shortest and sternest OT book of prophesy recorded. Nothing is known of the author, although his prophecy is against Edom, Israel's longstanding enemy. It is said to be composed sometime in the fifth century B.C. During this period, the Edomites had been forced to abandon their ancient home, and settled in southern Judah. The prophecy is a bitter cry for vengeance against Edom. The mountain of Esau will be occupied and ravaged by the enemy, but Zion shall remain safe and unchanged. Judah and Israel shall again form one nation. Many of the verses in this prophesy parallel to Jeremiah 49:7-22.

The Prophet
Jonah

(The Consequence of a Vindictive and Disobedience Prophets)

Historical Summary
JONAH (joh'nuh) Personal name meaning "dove"

Written probably in the fifth century B.C., this book is a didactic or moralistic story with an important theological message. It concerns a disobedient, self-righteous, and vindictive prophet who attempted to run away from his divine commission. Upon escaping on a ship, he was cast overboard and swallowed by a great fish, rescued in a marvelous manner, and sent on his way to Nineveh, a long-standing enemy of Israel. The wicked and evil city listened to his message of doom and repented immediately. God did not carry out the punishment he had planned for them. Afterward, Jonah complained to God. He was bitter because he wanted God to destroy Israel's enemies, rather than to forgive them. From this story, a basic lesson can be drawn. Jonah's vindictive mentality creates a direct conflict with the mercy of God. This prophecy is a parable of mercy. The book has also prepared the way for the gospel with its message of redemption for all, both Jew and Gentile.

The Prophet
Micah

(Fought Rich Exploiters of the Poor, False Prophets, Bribery, and fraud)

Historical Summary
MICAH (mi'/cuh) Abbreviated form of Micaiah, meaning, "Who is like Yahweh?"

Micah came from an unknown village of Moresheth (inheritance of the winepress) in the foothills. With eloquent speech he attacked the rich exploiters of the poor, fraudulent merchants, carnal judges, corrupt priests and false prophets. Both Samaria and Jerusalem were singled out for judgment. Jeremiah 26:17-18 informs us that the preaching of Micah influenced the reform of Hezekiah. The prophecy may be divided into three parts: 1. The impending judgment and criticism of Judah's leaders for betrayal of their responsibility (Micah 1:1-3:12). 2. The glory of the restored Zion. A reunited Israel. (Micah 4:1-5:14). 3. The case against Israel. The picture closes with a prayer for national restoration and an expression of trust in God's mercy (Micah 6:1-7:20). Each of these three parts start with reproach and the threat of punishment, and ends on a note of hope and promise.

The Prophet
Nahum

(Prophesied the Unrestrained Vengeance of God)

Historical Summary
NAHUM (nay'/huhm) Personal name meaning, "comfort, and encourage."

Shortly before the fall of Nineveh in 612 B.C., Nahum prophesied against the city. In the wake of their conquests, mounds of heads, dead bodies, enslaved citizens, and greedy looters testified to the ruthlessness of the Assyrians. This is why Judah joined in the general outburst of joy over the destruction of Nineveh. Nahum is not a prophet of unrestrained revenge. God's moral government of the world is defined. God is the avenger, but he is also the Merciful One, a stronghold in the day of distress. Nineveh's doom was a judgment on the wicked city. The Book is divided in two parts: 1. The Lord's coming in Judgment (Nahum 1:2 – 2:1-3); and 2. The fall of Nineveh (Nahum 2:2 – 3:19).

The Prophet
Habakkuk
(Questions God about the Enemies of Judah)

Historical Summary
HABAKKUK (huh'/bak/'kuhk) personal name based on a root meaning "to embrace."

This prophecy dates from the years 605-597 B.C. Judah was desperate at this time, with political intrigue and idolatry widespread in the kingdom. The first two chapters consist of a dialogue between the prophet and the Lord. For the first time in canonical literature, a man humbly questions the ways of God. Habakkuk asked God to give an account for his government of the world. To this question, God replies that he has prepared a chastising rod, Babylon, which will be the avenging instrument in his hand. The third chapter is a magnificent religious lyric, filled with reminiscences of Israel's past. It also borrowers a lot of poetic literature from ancient Canaan, though still expressing authentic Israelite faith. God appears in *His* entire majestic splendor and then executes vengeance on Judah's enemies. The prophecy ends with a joyous profession of confidence in the Lord.

The Prophet
Zephaniah

(Protested Worship of False gods, condemned pro-Assyrian Ministers)

Historical Summary
ZEPHANIAH (zehf/uh/ni'/uh) Personal name meaning, "Yahweh sheltered or stored up" or "Zaphon (God is Yahweh)."

_____

The nature of this prophesy informs us that the ministry of Zephaniah took place during the reign of Josiah (640-609 B.C.). The protest against the worship of false gods, and the condemnation of the pro-Assyrian ministers, allow us to place the work in the first decade of Josiah's reign. The prophesy of Zephaniah was a time of religious degradation, when old idolatries reappeared and men worshipped the sun, moon, and stars. To the corrupt city, Zephaniah announced the approaching judgment of the day of the Lord. **The prophesy is divided into three sections, which correspond to the three chapters of the book: 1. A day of doom. 2. A Day of Judgment for the enemies of God's people (Zephaniah 2:1-15). 3. Reproach and promise for Jerusalem. Despite Judah's infidelities, the Lord's mercy will spare a holy remnant, which will finally enjoy peace.** The prophesy closes with a hymn of joy sung by the remnant restored to Zion (Zephaniah 3:1-20).

The Prophet
Haggai
(Exhorted Israelites to Rebuild)

Historical Summary

HAGGAI (hag'/gah/ee) Personal name of a sixth century prophet meaning, "Festive."

Post-exilic prophesy begins with Haggai in 520 B.C. The Jews who returned from the exile in Babylonia had encountered obstacles in their efforts to re-establish Jewish life in Judah. The Samaritans blocked the rebuilding of the temple; but after Darius took over the throne 522 B.C., permission was given to resume the work. At this moment, when the people were defeated and sluggish, Haggai came forward with his exhortations. The first prophesy, an appeal to the Jews, is contained in Haggai chapter 1. To this appeal Haggai added a short prophesy of encouragement (Haggai 2:1-9). The prophesy may be divided into five parts: 1. The call to rebuild the temple. The economic distress in Judah is due to the Jews' neglect of the Lord while they provide for their own needs (Haggai 1: 1-15). 2. The future glory of the new temple, surpassing that of the old (Haggai 2:1-9). 3. Unworthiness of a people, who may be the Samaritans, to offer sacrifice at the newly restored altar. This prophesy is cast in the literary form of a Torah; an instruction given to the people by a priest (Haggai 2:10-14). 4. A promise of immediate blessings, which follows upon the undertaking (Hag 1) to rebuild the temple (Haggai 2:15-19). 5. A pledge to Zerubbabel, descendant of David, one of the messianic hopes (Haggai 2:20-23).

The Prophet
Zechariah
(Encouraged Returning Exiles to Rebuild)

Historical Summary
ZECHARIAH (zehk/uh/ri'/uh) Personal name meaning, "Yah remembered."

Zechariah's initial prophesy is dated to 520 B.C., the same year that Haggai received his prophetic call. The first eight chapters of the Book of Zechariah contain prophecies that belong to him, while the last six (sometimes called "Deutero-Zechariah") represent the work of one or more unknown authors. In the prophecies proper to Zechariah, eight symbolic visions are recorded. All eight are meant to promote the work of rebuilding the temple to encourage the returned exiles, especially their leaders, Joshua and Zerubbabel. In the final chapter of this first division, Zechariah portrays the messianic future under the figure of a prosperous land. The second part of Zechariah is divided into two sections. The first, Zechariah 9-11 consists of prophecies whose historical background, date and authorship are difficult to determine. With the messianic vision of the coming of the Prince of Peace in Zechariah 9:9. The verses describing the triumphant appearance of the humble king are taken up by the four Evangelists to describe the entry of Christ into Jerusalem on Palm Sunday. Zechariah chapter 12 is introduced by an prophesy proclaiming the victory of God's people over the heathen. The prophesy closes by describing in apocalyptic imagery, the final assault of the enemy on Jerusalem, after which the messianic age begins.

The Prophet
Malachi
(Unknown Author name meaning:
"My Messenger" Reproaches Priests and Rulers)

Historical Summary
MALACHI (mal/'uh/ki) Common noun meaning, "my messenger," or "my angel"

This is the work an anonymous writer shortly before Nehemiah's arrival in Jerusalem (445 B.C.). As a result of his sharp reproaches against the priests and rulers, the author probably wished to conceal his identity. To do this he made a proper name out of the Hebrew expression for "My Messenger" (Malachi), which occurs in (Malachi 1:1, 3:1). The historical value of the prophesy is considerable in that it gives us a picture of life in the Jewish community returned from Babylon, between the period of Haggai and the reform of Ezra and Nehemiah. It is likely that the author's cutting criticism of abuses by religious leaders prepared the way for necessary reforms. The priests dishonored God with their blemished sacrifices. In the first chapter, the writer foresees the time when all nations will offer a pure sacrifice (Malachi 1:11). The prophecies fulfillment in seen in the sacrifice of the sacrament of Christ. Afterward, the author turns from the priest to the people, denouncing their marriages with pagans, and rebuking their heartless denial of Israelite wives. Due to the critical spirit of the times, many grew weary and questioned God,

"Where is the God of justice?" To this question the prophet replies that the day of the Lord is coming. First, the forerunner must come, who will prepare the soil for repentance and true worship. The Gospel writers point to John the Baptist as the forerunner ushering in the messianic age. When the ground is prepared, God will appear, measuring out rewards and punishments and purifying the nation in the furnace of judgment. He will create a new order in which the ultimate triumph of good is inevitable.

Section II

THE PLOT OF THE PROPHETS
The Fellowship of Suffering and Timeline Chart

Summation of Biblical Themes of the Prophetic Office

PROPHET	NAME MEANING	SUMMATION OF SUFFERING
1. Isaiah	Yahweh Saves	Rejection
2. Jeremiah	Yahweh Lift Up	Arrest, Imprisonment, and Public Disgrace
3. Ezekiel	God will Strengthen	First known prophet called in Babylon
4. Daniel	God is Judge	Author unknown, named after a Hebrew Patriarch
5. Hosea	Salvation	Married a prostitute to display and empathize with God's compassion
6. Joel	Yah is God	Frightened by what he witnessed
7. Amos	A Load	Expelled from the royal sanctuary
8. Obadiah	Yahweh's Servant	Wrote the shortest and sternest Prophesy
9. Jonah	Dove	Self-righteous, vindictive, and Disobedient
10. Micah	Who is Like Yahweh	Fought rich exploiters of the poor, false prophets, bribery, and fraud.
11. Nahum	Comfort/Encourage	Prophesied God's unrestrained Vengeance
12. Habakkuk	To Embrace	Questioned God about the enemies of Judah
13. Zephaniah	Yahweh Stored Up Or Sheltered	Protested the worship of false gods
14. Haggai	Festive	Exhorted Israelites to rebuild
15. Zechariah	Yah Remembered	Exhorted exiles to rebuild
16. Malachi	My Messenger	Unknown author reproached priests and rulers

Chronological Listing of Prophetic Books

PROPHETS	APPROXIMATE DATES OF PROPHETIC LITERATURE
OBADIAH	845 – 840 B.C.
JOEL	835 B.C.
JONAH	786 – 746 B.C.
AMOS	750 – 749 B.C.
ISAIAH	740 – 701 B.C.
HOSEA	760 – 720 B.C.
MICAH	735 – 700 B.C.
ZEPHANIAH	640 – 609 B.C.
NAHUM	612 B.C.
JEREMIAH	627 – 630 B.C.
LAMENTATIONS	628 – 587 B.C.
HABAKKUK	605 – 597 B.C.
EZEKIEL	597 B.C.
HAGGAI	520 B.C.
ZECHARIAH	520 – 470 B.C.
MALACHI	445 – 440 B.C.
DANIEL	167- 164 B.C.

Prophets often glean from one another's writings and attended informal schools of prophesy, (i.e. see Gilgal). As a result, it is very helpful to understand the chronological order in which the books were written. Based on recent archeological finds, scholars believe that Gilgal was not a specific geographical location. It signifies the religious beliefs and teachings that introduce us to a spiritual life. Therefore, many of the prophets shared ideas and advanced one another's work. The significance of understanding the chronological order of these books reflects how each prophet gleaned from prior literature to echo the voice of Yah.

The Bible is often divided into 5 parts: 1. The Pentateuch, 2. Historical Books, Poetic and Wisdom Writings, 3. Major Prophets, 4. Minor Prophets, and 5. New Testament Writings.

There are other prophets mentioned throughout scripture that are not considered "literary prophets." Various prophets have no personally written literature. However, their impact and existence is thoroughly mentioned throughout each part of the Bible. For example, the prophets Eli, Samuel, Nathan, Elijah, Elisha, Obed, Jesus Christ, and other prophets are referenced throughout the 66 canonical books of the Bible, but they simply have no known recorded writings of their own.

THE SOLEMN AND SACRED CREED

The Prophets Doctrine

The Solemn and Sacred Creed

A prophet is a poetic voice that speaks pertaining to prophecies, dreams, visions, revelation, forewarnings, and predictions. Prophets are seers that are loyal to the purpose of God. They oftentimes encounter rejection, experience arrests, endure imprisonments, and suffer public disgrace. Prophets we are agents of Zion, assigned to God's people despite physical location or spiritual condition. Prophets display God's compassion. Prophets are enlightened and even frightened by what is seen spiritually, specifically visions that are unlawful to utter with words. Prophets expect persecution and being ousted for sharp judgment. Prophets speak short and stern statements. They fight rich exploiters of the poor, false prophets, judges that take bribes, and fraudulent behavior – they prophesy the unrestrained vengeance of God. Prophets consistently seek wisdom from God alone. Prophets protest the worship of false gods as well as ministers of unrighteousness. They exhort and encourage God's people to repent and rebuild. Prophets bring reproach on corrupt priests, pastors, and wayward rulers. Prophets are seers serving as the mouthpiece of God; therefore, they revive and preserve His word in the earth. Prophets are chosen to serve as messengers of the Most-High God.

MORE THAN A FORTUNE-TELLER
Responsibilities of a Prophet

WHAT THE BIBLE SAYS ABOUT TRUE PROPHETS

PROPHETS OPEN BLINDED EYES: THEY ENABLE PEOPLE TO ENTER KNEW DIMENSIONS OF LIFE.
"They say unto the blind man again, What says thou of him, that he hath opened thine eyes? He said, He is a prophet" **(John 9:17).**

PROPHETS LIVE IN DIMENSIONS THAT OTHERS ARE UNABLE TO OPERATE IN. *"And said unto Jeremiah the prophet, Let, we beseech thee, our supplication be accepted before thee, and pray for us unto the Lord thy God, even for all this remnant; for we are left but a few of many, as thine eyes do behold us"* **(Jeremiah 42:2).**

PROPHETS SEE INTO THE SPIRIT REALM. *"We see not our signs: there is no more any prophet: neither is there among us any that knoweth how long"* **(Psalms 74:9).**

A PROPHET IS GOD'S MOUTHPIECE AND SEER. *There are two Hebrew words for prophet or perhaps even two types of prophets. The Hebrew words for prophet are "Heb nabi" which means to bubble forth or to utter, and "ro'eh" which means seer.*

PROPHETS ARE INDIVIDUALS WHO SEE INTO THE FUTURE. *"Beforetime, in Israel, when a man went to inquire of God, thus he spoke, Come, and let us go to the seer: for he that is now called a prophet was formerly called a seer"* **(I Samuel 9:9).**

PROPHETS ARE PRE-POSITIONED TO TRANSITION GOD'S PEOPLE INTO HIS PREORDAINED PURPOSE. GOD USES PROPHETS TO CHANGE REALITY, AS WE KNOW IT. *"Surely the Lord GOD will do nothing, but he revealeth his secret unto his servants the prophets"* **(Amos 3:7).**

PROPHETS MUST ACCEPT THE BURDENSOME RESPONSIBILITY TO SUFFER FOR GOD. *"The burden which Habakkuk the prophet did see"* **(Habakkuk 1:1).**

PROPHETS MUST BE WILLING TO ENDURE PERSECUTION UNTIL AN ASSIGNMENT IS COMPLETE. *"Rejoice, and be exceeding glad: for great is your reward in heaven: for so persecuted they the prophets which were before you"* **(Matthew 5:12).**

PROPHETS IGNORE PHYSICAL MANIFESTATIONS. *"I made a covenant with mine eyes; why then should I think upon a maid"* **(Job 31:1)?**

PROPHETS HAVE HONOR. *"And they were offended in him. But Jesus said unto them, a prophet is not without honor, save in his own country, and in his own house"* **(Matthew 13:57).**

PROPHETS ARE KILLED FOR SAYING WHAT THEY SEE. *"Wherefore ye be witnesses unto yourselves, that ye are the children of them which killed the prophets"* **(Matthew 23:31).**

The Specific Responsibilities of a Prophet

There is a distinct difference between God sending angels, His Word, the seven Spirits, and prophets. God sends specific agents on specific assignments in order to accomplish a specific purpose. Prophets are seers that possess the secrets of God – they see into the timeless spirit-realm and prophesy concerning the future. Prophet do not focus on your past, unlike psychics. God sends prophets on assignments for the following reasons:

THE CALL (CAUSE)	THE ACTION (AFFECT)
1. Sent to suffer:	DECLARE or SACRIFICE
2. Sent to purge	WARNING/ADMONITION (Prior to Destruction)
3. Sent for preservation:	DISCRETION/CORRECTION
4. Sent to set free:	LIBERATE or COMFORT
5. Sent to remind:	RECOLLECTION/MEMORY

WARNING: Many false prophets will continue to attempt to deceive God's people for selfish gain, authority, and positions of influence. However, these general and specific responsibilities of a prophet will help readers to recognize the difference between true and false prophets. More importantly, this book will help you hear the voice of God without the unnecessary instrument of man serving as the mouthpiece.

The following scriptures capture the essence of God's warning against the dangers of false prophets:

CONSIDER YOURSELF WARNED

"Thus saith the Lord GOD; Woe unto the foolish prophets, that follow their own spirit, and have seen nothing" (**Ezekiel 13:3**)!

"Therefore prophesy against them, prophesy, O son of man" (**Ezekiel 11:4**).

"Son of man, prophesy against the prophets of Israel that prophesy, and say thou unto them that prophesy out of their man own hearts, Hear ye the word of the LORD" (**Ezekiel 13:2**).

"Woe unto them! For they have fled from me: destruction unto them! Because they have transgressed against me: though I have redeemed them, yet they have spoken lies against me" (**Hosea 7:13**).

"Woe unto you, when all men shall speak well of you! For so did their fathers to the false prophets" (**Luke 6:26**).

"Then the LORD said unto me, The prophets prophesy lies in my name: I sent them not, neither have I commanded them, neither spoke unto them: they prophesy unto you a false vision and divination, and a thing of naught, and the deceit of their heart" (**Jeremiah 14:14**).

"Beware of false prophets, which come to you in sheep's clothing, but inwardly they are ravening wolves" (**Matthew 7:15**).

"And many false prophets shall rise, and shall deceive many" (**Matthew 24:11**).

"For there shall arise false Christs, and false prophets, and shall show great signs and wonders; insomuch that, if it were possible, they shall deceive the very elect" (**Matthew 24:24**).

"And the king of Israel said unto Jehoshaphat, There is yet one man. Micaiah the son of Imlah, by whom we may inquire of the LORD: but I hate him; for he doth not prophesy good concerning me, but evil. And Jehoshaphat said, Let not the king say so" (**I Kings 22:8**).

"Which say to the seers, See not; and to the prophets, prophesy not unto us right things, speak unto us smooth things, prophesy deceits" (**Isaiah 30:10**).

"The prophets prophesy falsely, and the priests bear rule by their means; and my people love to have it so: and what will ye do in the end thereof" (**Jeremiah 5:31**)?

SEEING BENEATH THE SURFACE
The Meaningful Miracles of Elijah and Elisha

The 14 Recorded Miracles in the Prophetic Career of Elijah

(The biblical relevance of each miracle is stated underneath).

1. Causing the rain to cease for 3 ½ years (1Kings 17:1)

    Spiritual Relevance: Shutting the windows of heaven

2. Being fed by the ravens (1Kings 17:4)

    Spiritual Relevance: Comprehending the thoughts of God

3. Miracle of the barrel of meal and cruse of oil (1Kings 17:14)

    Spiritual Relevance: Possess an anointed word

4. Resurrection of the widow's son (1Kings 17:22)

    Spiritual Relevance: Revival of revelation

5. Calling of fire from heaven on the altar (1Kings 18:38)

    Spiritual Relevance: Possess the ability to purge

6. Causing it to rain (1Kings 18:45)

    Spiritual Relevance: Opening the windows of Heaven

7. Prophesy that Ahab's sons would all be destroyed (1Kings 21:22)

    Spiritual Relevance: Foresee the fate of sinners

8. Prophesy that Jezebel would be eaten by dogs (1Kings 21:23)

    Spiritual Relevance: Foresee the cruel fate of shameless sinners

9. Prophesy that Ahaziah would die of his illness (2Kings 1:4)

   Spiritual Relevance: Foresee how God holds firm

10. Calling fire from heaven upon the first 50 soldiers (2Kings 2:10)

    Spiritual Relevance: Command purging

11. Calling fire from heaven upon the second 50 soldiers (2Kings 2:12)

    Spiritual Relevance: Consistently command purging

12. Parting of the Jordan (2Kings 2:8)

    Spiritual Relevance: Rightly divide the Word

13. Prophesy Elisha's double portion of his spirit (2Kings 2:10)

    Spiritual Relevance: Speak Truths

14. Being caught up to heaven in a whirlwind (2Kings 2:11)

    Spiritual Relevance: Moved by the Spirit of God

The 28 Recorded Miracles in the Prophetic Career of Elisha

Study, examine and research for biblical context clues to define the spiritual relevance of each miracle. The Bible is filled with symbolisms, metaphors, and figurative language. Truth travels far beneath the surface of traditional thinking and physical manifestations. Revelation enables individuals to embrace a more objective, accurate, and meaningful understanding. Everything God does is done with purpose and specific intentions.

1.   Parting of the Jordan (2Kings 2:14)

2.   Healing of the waters (2Kings 2:21)

3.   Curse of the she bears (2Kings 2:24)

4.   Filling of the valley with water (2Kings 3:17)

5.   Deception of the Moabites with the valley of blood (2Kings 3:22)

6.   Miracle of the vessels of oil (2Kings 4:4)

7.   Prophesy that Shunammite woman would have a son (2Kings 4:16)

8.   Resurrection of the Shunammite's son (2Kings 4:34)

9.   Healing of the gourds (2Kings 4:41)

10.   Miracle of the bread (2Kings 4:43)

11.   Healing of Naaman (2Kings 5:14)

12.   Perception of Gehazi's transgression (2 Kings 5:26)

13.   Cursing Gehazi with leprosy (2 Kings 5:27)

14.   Floating of the axe head (2 Kings 6:6)

15.   Prophesy of the Syrian battle plans (2Kings 6:9)

16.   Vision of the chariots (2Kings 6:17)

17.   Smiting the Syrian army with blindness (2Kings 6:18)

18.   Restoring the sight of the Syrian army (2Kings 6:20)

19.   Prophesy of the end of the great famine (2Kings 7:1)

20.   Prophesy that the scoffing nobleman would see (2Kings 7:2)

21.   Deception of the Syrians with the sound of chariots (2Kings 7:6)

22.   Prophesy of the seven – year famine (2Kings 8:1)

23.   Prophesy of Benhadad's untimely death (2Kings 8:10)

24.   Prophesy of Hazael's cruelty to Israel (2Kings 8:12)

25.   Prophesy that Jehu would smite the house of Ahab
        (2Kings 9:7)

26.   Prophesy that Joash would smite the Syrains at Aphek
        (2Kings 13:17)

27.   Prophesy that Joash would smite Syria thrice (2Kings 13:19)

28.   Resurrection of the man touched by his bones (2Kings 13:21)

THE PROPHETESS

Females in Five-Fold Ministry

Can a Woman Serve as a Prophetess?

A woman can undoubtedly serve as a prophetess, (or any other speaking role in the church), despite chauvinistic influences that govern in religion. Let's consider what the Bible states about God speaking through female vessels. According to scripture, not to compare women to animals or inanimate objects, God even spoke through a donkey and rocks (See Numbers 22:28 and Luke 19:40). Unquestionably, God uses women as vessels to declare truth.

Keep in mind it is dangerously confusing when men or women forfeit their gender specific roles – and God is not the author of confusion. Women represent God's ability to manifest (See Genesis 3:16). Women represent the glory of men, the beauty of a relationship, and the helpmeet of their husbands. There are unequivocally physical differences between a man and a woman. Although, we must factor in the reality that we are more spiritual-beings than physical creatures. According to the Bible, *"There is neither Jew nor Greek, there is neither bond nor free, there is neither male nor female: for you are all one in Christ Jesus"* (Galatians 3:28).

In the beginning as the Bible portrays it, God gave Adam and Eve gender specific consequences for sin. Eve (the woman) travails in birth, and Adam (the man) suffers from thorns. The

Creator was very strategic upon creating both male and female. Neither vessel is greater or self-sustaining without the other. While women are the weaker vessel, they are by no means the lesser vessel. There is indeed a reason why the Apostle Paul instructed women not to teach in the churches.

I Corinthians 14:33–35 states, *"As in all the congregations of the saints, women should remain silent in the churches. They are not allowed to speak, but must be in submission, as the Law says. If they want to inquire about something, they should ask their own husbands at home; for it is disgraceful for a woman to speak in the church."* For some churches, that isolated verse is doctrine. However, earlier in the same letter to the church of Corinth (I Corinthians 11:5), Paul mentions women praying and prophesying as allowable activities. Women are also instructed to teach younger women (Titus 2:4). Therefore, 1 Corinthians 14:33–35 is not be an absolute command for women not to interact during the worship experience. Let's consider the history and some modern facts. The Corinthian church was known for chaos, lack of order, and uneducated women. NT believers are subject or accountable to the law. Today, women are not restrained to the circumstances that oppressed women from learning, advancing and speaking in churches.

With no uncertainty, Paul was very familiar with the prophecies and spiritual leadership of female patriarchs like Mirriam, Deborah, Huldah, Noadiah, and NT prophetess Anna.

Using multiple scriptures enable us to compare, contrast, and put Paul's words in the proper context. His discretion had everything to do with both, a seasonal and regional condition of blind-sided and weak believers failing to exercise order. When believers focus on manifestation with no regard to revelation, new doctrines are defined that do not reflect God's deliberate intentions.

As believers, we should never aim to learn, or base our realities on what we see or feel – this causes confusion (see I Co 2:13). Biases and subjective thinking are dangerously destructive with regards to how we see others. The word 'woman' is interchangeable with manifestation. Women are a visual of man's glory. Females are the only human vessels that have the ability to pro-create and re-produce. Equally as interesting, the 'Y' chromosome of the male determines the gender of an offspring. Opposite of women, men represent revelation. Revelation is the rock upon which God builds the church that manifests his glory.

The Greek word for church is *Ecclesia*, means "Called Out Ones", summoned or a governmental assembly. The kingdom of God is a domestic democracy, where both men and women serve distinct and different roles. Yet, women have full authority to speak on behalf of God in an assembly, especially when God Himself gives her a prophetic message. In addition, mature women should always speak into the lives of younger ladies. Manifestation is the result of revelation, therefore, women should submit to male authority, because God made man first, and the woman came from man, based on the Bible.

When women exert authority over men, it's like putting the carriage before the horse. Manifestation (women) is no less important than revelation (men), although things seen always support things that are not. Hence, the woman's first priority is to sustain life and support mankind. It is easy in modern society to misconstrue the significance of God's intention for creating males and *fe*males. Single fathers, unwed mothers, shifting responsibilities, and changing domestic roles can make this insight appear confusing. However, God's original intention remains unchanged. Alternative domestic lifestyles and modern work practices appear helpful and harmless, yet they are clearly born in dysfunction and remain unnatural. This reality is critical to fulfilling individual responsibilities in ministry. God's designed us on purpose with specific intentions, both spiritually and physically. Despite extreme feminist groups and male chauvinistic movements, we are all purposed with design. God has a distinct role for both men and women. Consider the following chart that lists women in the Bible that served significant speaking roles on behalf of God.

WOMEN WITH PUBLIC VOICES, WHOLESOME VIRTUE & SPIRITUAL VISION
Called-Out to Speak on God's Behalf (Romans 8:30)

MIRRIAM the prophetess
"And Miriam the prophetess, the sister of Aaron, took a timbrel in her hand; and all the women went out after her with timbrels and with dances" (Exodus 15:20).

DEBORAH the prophetess
"And Deborah, a prophetess, the wife of Lapidoth, she judged Israel at that time" (Judges 4:4).

HULDAH the prophetess
"And Hilkiah, and they that the king had appointed, went to Huldah the prophetess, the wife of Shallum the son of Tikvath, the son of Hasrah, keeper of the wardrobe; (now she dwealt in Jerusalem in the college:) and they spoke to her that effect" (II Chronicles 34:22).

NOADIAH the prophetess
"My God, think upon Tobiah and Sanballat according to these their works, and other prophetess Noadiah, and the rest of the prophets, that would have put me in fear" (Nehemiah 6:1-19).

ANNA the prophetess
"And there was one Anna, a prophetess, the daughter of Phanuel, of the tribe of Asher: she was of a great age, and had lived with a husband seven years from her virginity" (Luke 2:36).

FALSE PROPHETS

Identifying Wolves Disguised in Sheep Clothing

Witchcraft is the sin of rebellion. Rebellion means to draw back and disobey by an act of violent or open resistance to an established government or ruler. Rebellion is also defined a control or manipulation. The enemy is often disguised as witches, warlocks, false prophets, sorcerers, psychics, and palm readers. These are all individuals who practice sorcery to influence fate or fortune. They aim to predict the future based on manipulation of information while imprisoning people to evidence of their past. On the other hand, a true prophet is a seer that holds sound doctrine in the highest regard. Prophets see into the future, through dreams and visions, based on God alone. According to I Samuel 15:23, "*For rebellion is as the sin of witchcraft, and stubbornness is as iniquity and idolatry.*" *Because thou hast rejected the word of the LORD, he hath also rejected thee from being king.*

Sorcerers, witches, warlocks, psychics and palm readers are all different titles for the antics used by false prophets. In essence, these ungodly practices are often leading influences in today's churches. The intent of false prophesy is to distract the hearers with physical possessions and turn listeners away from the faith. According to Acts 13:6-8, *And when they had gone through the isle unto Paphos, they found a certain sorcerer, a false prophet, a Jew, whose name was Barjesus: Which was with the deputy of the country, Sergius Paulus, a prudent man; who called for Barnabas and Saul, and desired to hear the word of God. But Elymas the sorcerer (for so is his name by interpretation) withstood them, seeking to turn away the deputy from the faith.*

Ministers should be positive, never negative. Although false prophets will always have something good and promising to say, as opposed to constructive guidance. They will aim to control you and your life through the weapon of fear or manipulation. According to I Kings 22:8, *And the king of Israel said unto Jehoshaphat, There is yet one man, Micaiah the son of Imlah, by whom we may inquire of the LORD: but I hate him; for he doth not prophesy good concerning me, but evil. And Jehoshaphat said, Let not the king say so.*

False prophets are wolves disguised as sheep. Therefore, false prophets will always make their prophesies contingent upon obedience for personal gain and influence, i.e. money, gifts, position, authority, etc. According to Matthew 7:15, *Beware of false prophets, which come to you in sheep's clothing, but inwardly they are ravening wolves.*

False prophets are used by Satan to deceive. God's prophets are used by God to enlighten. Deception is dangerous, because it is the spellbound mixture of many facts and scriptures, but still void of the truth. The aim of a false prophet is to deceive the masses with the most manipulative tricks and schemes. People who do not study and pray are easily beguiled, tricked, and misled. According to Matthew 24:24, *"For there shall arise false Christs, and false prophets, and shall show great signs and wonders; insomuch that, if it were possible, they shall deceive they very elect."*

False prophets also have the ability to display signs and wonders, and they validate their ministry based on these signs. Remember only a wicked and perverse generation seeks after a sign. Never focus on signs. My book *Seed-Time, Liberating the Oppressed*, is a phenomenal book to gain a clear insight on distinguishing the significance between spiritual promises vs. physical things. According to Mark 13:22, *"For false Christs and false prophets shall rise, and shall show signs and wonders, to seduce, if it were possible, even the elect."*

False prophets specialize in operating in sensationalism. They inspire the masses with music, prey on the emotionally weak with eloquent speech, and use past tragedies to speak into the future of broken-hearted people. Know this, God is more concerned about your soul, than the house you live in, or the car you drive. God does not make material promises to people who are dying spiritually. God does not elevate individuals who are spiritually dead. God's message (prophecy) to sinners has remained the same since Christ, *"Repent: for the kingdom of heaven is at hand"* (Matthew 4:17).

FALSE PROPHETS RECORDED IN THE BIBLE

(There are other false prophets that are not referenced by name)

FALSE PROPHETS NAMED	BIBLICAL REFERENCE
Ahab	Jeremiah 29:21
Elymasor Bar-Jesus	Acts 13:6-12
Pashhur	Jeremiah 20:6
Hananiah	Jeremiah 28:5-16
Zedekiah	I kings 22:11
Shemaiah	Jeremiah 29:24-32
Balaam	II Peter 2:15-16

FALSE PROPHETS UNNAMED	BIBLICAL REFERENCE
The False Prophet of Revelation	Revelation 16:3
The 450 False Prophets of Baal	I Kings 18:19-20
The 400 False Prophets of Asherah	I Kings 18:19-20
Ahab's Prophets	I Kings 22:10-12
More Prophets of Baal	Jeremiah 2:8/23:13

MODERN-DAY PROPHESY
New Covenant Prophets in the New Testament

THE ORIGIN OF THE MINISTRY OF PROPHESY
(Genesis 20:1-7, Exodus 20:1-19 and Deuteronomy 18:15-22)

God instituted the Office of the prophet in response to the Children of Israel. They feared the voice of the Lord, but would only hear the words of men. Therefore, Yah raised up Prophets from among His people. Initially, a prophet was one who heard from God, as a father, on behalf of his family or kinsmen.

THE NEW TESTAMENT CHURCH
(See Joel 2:28-32)

The gift was promised to the Church as an ongoing ministry in the New Testament. (*See: Romans 12:6, 1 Corinthians 12:10, 1 Corinthians 14:1-5, and Ephesians 4:11)* Paul also places an importance on the operation within the Church.

THE PURPOSE OF THE PROPHET

The enduring purpose of the Prophetic Ministry is to serve as God's Spokesman in all ages. (Genesis 20:1-7, Ephesians 4:11).

CHECKS AND CONTROLS ON PROPHETS

There are four basic controls over the operation of a Prophet's ministry as outlined in the Word:

1. The Lord Himself (Deuteronomy 18:22, Ephesians 1:22).
2. Other Ministries (Hebrews 13:7). Note: It should be noted that Pastors and Elders are also subject to the Prophetic Ministry as well, because they are subject to the Rhema Word of God, which came by the mouth of the Prophets (2 Peter 1:19-21).

3. Other Prophets (1 Corinthians 14:29, 32).
4. The Body (Church) as a whole (Ephesians 5:21).

THE FUNCTION OF THE PROPHET IN THE CHURCH

A). To build up the Church in Faith, hope and love (I Corinthians 14:3-4, 22).

B). To lay open the secrets of the hearts of men (1 Corinthians 14:25)

C). To convict and judge unbelievers (I Corinthians 14:24)

D). To verify the Word of the Lord to both the Church and to individuals (I Corinthians 14:29, 37).

E). To be an instrument of on-going revelation to the Body (Matthew 16:18, Ephesians
2:20, Ephesians 3:5)

F). To bring warnings from God and to foreshadow His actions in the Church (Amos 3:7, Acts 21:11)

G). To call other ministries and confirm their appointment from the Lord (I Samuel 10:1, Acts 13:1-13).

H). To give on-going direction to other ministries as the Lord sees fit (Acts 16:6, Acts 20:23, 1 Timothy 1:18).

I). To command the seven spirits of God in the earthly domain (see Isaiah 45:11 and I Corinthians 14:32).

LIMITATIONS ON THE OFFICE OF THE PROPHET

There are three known basic limitations on the operation of the gift and ministry of prophets:

1. The Proportion of Faith (Romans 12:6).
2. The Lack of Love (1 Corinthians 13:2).
3. We Know in Part (1 Corinthians 13:9).

SCRIPTURAL EXAMPLES OF PROPHETS IN THE MINISTRY

Some examples of the ministry of Prophets in the New Testament are: (See: Acts 11:27-28, Acts 13:1, Acts 15:32, Acts 21:10-11). The Prophet expresses a very important role in the Body of believers and requires constant refining and humility.

THE LIFESTYLE OF A PROPHET
Mastering the Art of Consecration, Isolation, and Meditation

The prophet must remain consecrated in effort to be used at God's disposal. Humility is vital to operate in the Spirit. The Prophet will be a broken man. He or she will often walk alone. They will be misunderstood. They will be tried and proven through tribulation and suffering. The Prophet will be a man or woman "acquainted with sorrow" because he will share in the fellowship of Christ's sufferings.

The office of the prophet requires an individual who has been totally consumed by God's Spirit and presence. Prophets are familiar with the wilderness experience. Prophets also have an endowment of authority from the Lord, expressing in the Body the Divine Holiness of God. Yah creates new things based on the Words spoken by a Prophet. For example, the Prophet confirms the "call" to ministry (1 Sam 10:1; Acts 13:1-3).

God uses the willingness and words spoken by prophets to unleash his divine will. "The Lord does nothing without first telling his servants the prophets" (Amos 3:7). The Prophet also gives direction and rebuke to individuals within the Body (II Samuel 12:1-12).

The ultimate example for prophets is Christ, who is the Word of God made flesh (John 1:14). The purpose of the prophetic office is to express within the Body of Christ the divine word in our human experience.

Section X

THE PROPHET IN THE CHURCH
Few Are Chosen

It is of critical importance that prophets understand the significant contrast between the church and the temple. Remember, the word church is Greek for ecclesia. In essence, it is the government of God, those that are "Called Out." It is derived from the Greek word ek-kaleo, which was used for the summons to the army to assemble. Christ said, *"And I say also unto thee, that thou art Peter, and upon this rock I will build my church; and the gates of hell shall not prevail against it"* (Matthew 16:18).

The Son of God came to establish a spiritual government that is not, and will never be of this world. He came preaching only one message, *"Repent for the kingdom of God is at hand."* The definition of the word repent means to literally change the way you've been thinking. In order to embrace the government of God or the church, we must attain a higher level of thought or meditation. Mankind has misrepresented and misconstrued the true meaning of the church. We've defined hierarchies, monopolies, and circles of self-gain as God's intent for qualifying individuals, religious groups, other sects, and races of people. Today, modern assemblies are open sores of misunderstanding and deception. The difference, or contrast, of a church as opposed to a temple is simple. The church is God's government, not a building made with hands. The temple is where God's Spirit dwells. Individual believers are the temples of God (see Mark 14:58 and Acts 7:48). The apostle Paul said, *"And what agreement hath the temple of God with idols? For ye are the temple of the living God; as God hath said, I will dwell in them, and walk in them; and I will be their God, and they shall be my people"* (II Corinthians 6:16). Also, Christ spoke of his own body as the temple in the writings of John 2:21, *"But he spoke of the temple of his body."* Jews, who have not accepted Christ as the savior, continue to identify the place of assembly as a synagogue, or the temple. Despite OT temples, the NT church was not established until the bloodshed of Christ. Therefore, under the new blood covenant, Christians are the temples of God.

If and when prophets seek validation from community leaders who think churches are just buildings, the office of the prophet becomes contaminated and controlled. God alone must be hallowed as your covering, your shelter, your hiding place, and your place of refuge.

People will unconsciously and even maliciously speak all manner of evil against you. They will lie concerning you with hopes of discrediting your ministry. They will use your past to attempt to assassinate your future. They will alter your intentions and manipulate the truth to revile you. Nonetheless, the government of God's kingdom is a domain that is officiated by His divine sovereignty alone. God established 5-fold-ministry for His government. Five-fold ministry is not to fulfill any earthly agenda of men who seek materialism and sensationalism. Prophets, apostles, evangelists, teachers, and pastors must understand the difference between the celestial government of the church of God, compared to the terrestrial assembly of men.

The office of the prophet is a difficult call. Prophets deliver messages that are often unwanted and unpopular. Prophets must remain consecrated enough to see what God desires, and to hear what God is saying. Remember, God speaks with a *still small voice* (I Kings 19:12). The greatest characteristics of God's voice are that it is still and small. Unlike physical beings, God is a Spirit (see John 4:24). Spirits do not possess a physical larynx. The larynx controls our vocal tone and speech. It is the cartilaginous structure often referred to as the voice box. The larynx operates based on vibrations that travel from one destination to another. It is the most significant and powerful form of human energy, spoken by one and heard by another. On the other hand, God's voice resonates from an inner source that requires neither motion nor vibration. God speaks within the hearts of men. The only way people will hear from God is consciously meditate and listen to his voice. Consistently hearing this still small voice requires an intentional effort and a consecrated lifestyle.

Prophets must surround themselves with like-minded individuals, and engulf themselves in truth. Prophets will experience the kind of loneliness and lowliness that feels like suffering. God desires to take every prophet through the process of enduring the most difficult kinds of pressure. The greater you press the more distinct the anointing you will experience. Finally, as a prophet, your service is to God alone. You will be despised, rejected, a person of sorrow acquainted with grief, and seldom esteemed (see Isaiah 53:3).

Now that you've been equipped, always know there is a reason for suffering. Be prepared to embrace it. A bodybuilder invokes added resistance to build strength, endurance, and muscle. Likewise, suffering makes us better, stronger, and more purpose driven. Suffering is usually unwanted, but I assure you that it is needed to ascertain higher heights. Believe it or not, God requires us to suffer, contrary to modern messages. Suffering empowers us to reap the benefits of breakthrough (I Peter 5:10). In fact, suffering is a biblical prerequisite of knowing God, fellowshipping with Him, and walking in His promises. If no suffering is involved, then no promises should be expected. Likewise, if no suffering is involved then the message nor the messenger were sent by God. Discerning the voice of God and/or understanding the pathways to prophesy is necessary for all believers. We should consistently present petitions before God, with our primary and most fulfilling request being, *"Speak to My Heart"*.

www.ingramcontent.com/pod-product-compliance
Lightning Source LLC
Chambersburg PA
CBHW031146090426
42738CB00008B/1238